LET'S GO,
TRUCKS!

by David L. Harrison

illustrated by Bill Dugan

A GOLDEN BOOK • NEW YORK
Western Publishing Company, Inc.
Racine, Wisconsin 53404

D1313795

Big trucks, little trucks, loud ones, quiet ones.
All kinds of trucks for all kinds of jobs. The trucks
are rolling! Here they come!

What has twelve tails, one horn, and squeals?
A dozen pigs in a livestock truck. These busy
trucks haul sheep, pigs, horses, and cows from
the farm to the market.

Round and round, the mixer's turning.
Round and round, the concrete's churning.
Rumble, rumble, turn and tumble.
Concrete mixer trucks are coming.

Turtles don't have sinks, stoves, ice chests, storage bins, tables, benches, or beds inside their shells as campers do. It's too bad turtles can't have campers.

Moving to Kalamazoo? You need a moving van. Everything from beds to sleds is packed and stacked and tied inside. In Kalamazoo you'll find your things there, too.

Ummmm! Warm bread! Fresh from the oven, the loaves are popped into the bread truck and rushed to stores all over town, so you can get a bit of better bread for your butter.

What do tanker trucks carry? Peanuts, gasoline. Oil, syrup, kerosene. Flour, tar, milk to drink. Wax, paint, and even ink. Lots of other liquids, too. That's what tankers carry.

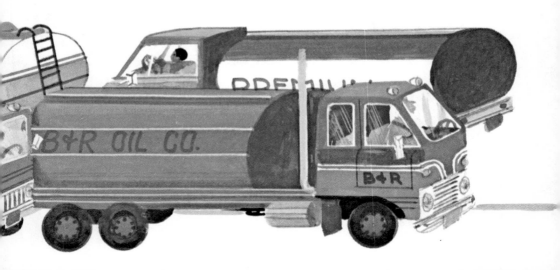

The trash truck crunches trash
and packs it tight with metal paddles.
Hold your ears! The trash truck eats trash
with a hungry roar!

The dogcatcher is catching dogs.
Bowwow! Bowwow! All you puppies
better hide. Find someplace to slip
inside, or you'll be taken for a ride!
Bowwow! Bowwow!

How do you haul 500 quarts of raspberry sherbet across a desert? In a refrigerator truck. It's frosty enough inside to please a polar bear, but polar bears aren't allowed. They might eat the raspberry sherbet!

Tow trucks tow cars. Tow trucks tow trucks. Tow trucks tow tow trucks. There's not much that tow trucks don't tow.

AL'S GARAGE

Up and up goes the utility truck. The cars are all honking. The red light is stuck.

Down and down goes the well-driller's drill.
The cows are all bawling for the new well to fill.

What do you haul in trailer trucks? Carpets, chairs, and teddy bears. Pots and pans and hats and fans. Sofas, suits, and cowboy boots. Almost anything at all is hauled in trailer trucks.

Bells ringing. Boys and girls shouting. Moms poking in their purses. Everybody's favorite truck is ding-a-linging down the street!

This is the mighty flatbed truck that hauled the steam shovel that never got stuck that worked on the road all smooth and new that carries the cars to Springtown.

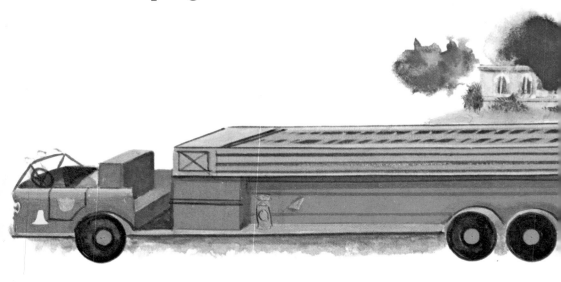

Cut off the siren! Unreel the hose! The fire's roaring! Pour on the water! The fire's sizzling. Pour on the water! The fire's hissing. Pour on the water! The fire's out. Let's all go home.

Stacks and sacks of money ride inside an armored truck. That's why the truck carries guards who carry guns. Crafty criminals and crooks can't crack into armored trucks.

A farmer's truck can deliver eggs, yank up a
stump, or haul hay to the horses. It can even turn
into a fruit stand! Fresh strawberries here!

Delivery trucks delivering. Beep, beep! Beep,
beep! Almost anything you wish. Flowers. Mail.
Laundry. Fish. Boxes. Baskets. Socks and bags.
Beep, beep!

Have a heavy load to haul? Call a dump truck.
Put it in. Haul it away. Tip it up. Dump it out.
Want to haul a hill away? Call a dump truck.

People make wishes when a transport trailer rolls by. "Aren't they beauties? Aren't they fine? Wish that one of those cars were mine!" People make wishes when a transport trailer rolls by.